CW01149414

BOOK SIGNING PAGE

TO: _____

And they overcame him by the blood of the Lamb and by the word of their testimony, and they did not love their lives to death.
(Revelation 12:11 NKJV)

Signature _____

The Blue Room:

If Walls Could Talk

by
Rev. Geraldine Callahan & Tjuana L. Callahan

The Blue Room: If Walls Could Talk

ladawn_3@yahoo.com
www.ladawnspeaks.com
IG @poetrybyladawn
FB @Ladawn Speaks
YouTube @ladawnspeaks3473

Copyright © 2024 by Rev. Geraldine Callahan and Tjuana L. Callahan

All rights reserved. Without written permission from the author, no part of this book may be reproduced or transmitted in any form or by any means, mechanical, electronic, video or audio recording, photocopying or by any information retrieval or storage system, except brief quotes for research, critical reviews, and articles.

Photos: Family Photo Album

ISBN: 979-8-9918386-0-3

Library of Congress Control Number: 2024923210

Published by G Publishing LLC
Huntsville, Alabama

The Blue Room: If Walls Could Talk
First Edition · First Printing
Memoir · Inspirational · Religion

Printed in the United States of America

DEDICATION

Giving all honor and praises to Father God Almighty!

I dedicate this book to the memory of my beloved parents, Erma & Grady Burley, and my play mothers Birdell Carter, and Grace Burnette. To my lifelong friends the "Quadells": Janet Carter White, Carol Carter, and Sandra Burnette White.

TABLE OF CONTENTS

	Introduction	9
	SECTION ONE - BEFORE THE BLUE ROOM	12
1	Way Back When	13
2	The Cover Up	18
3	Trials and Tribulations	21
4	A Time of Reckoning	28
	SECTION TWO – THE BLUE ROOM	31
5	His Plan, His Purpose	32
6	Saved from Stardom	37
7	The School of Hard Knocks	51
8	End the Beginning	55
	SECTION THREE – BEYOND THE BLUE ROOM	59
9	Love at First Sight?	60
10	My Three Girls	64
11	The Great Escape	69
12	Destiny Meets Purpose	74
	About the Authors	89
	Other Books by the Authors	90
	Picture References	91

INTRODUCTION

It is my desire to pique the depth of your spiritual soul's connection to our culture and history, to our connection with God and to our very present existence. To read this written account without being personally affected by its message might indicate some level of denial. To move forward we must face reality. Truth provides breakthrough of purpose and destiny. Therefore, my presentation comes to you with twinges of my own personal testimony woven throughout.

As I prepared to articulate my very personal testimony, I found my life flashing before my eyes, with some gut-wrenching realities, as well as blessings through the awesome resolve of God. In sharing, you may hear overtones of sarcasm, yet right around the corner of that emotion comes freedom to let go of that "closet type bondage mentality." Perhaps, after examining my interpretation, you too, will gather the courage to search your innermost dwelling. It just may release you from those family traditions or skeletons (secrets) lurking in your closet of bondage.

Many times, there are family secrets hiding among themselves or behind closed doors. These hidden truths do exist in plain sight, but we can't see them. It is the author's intention to pique your interest by giving you some personal family history.

I found out for myself that if you want answers to questions, you may be looking in all the wrong places. What about hiding something in a dark, cold place such as a basement? But the basement wasn't the only place for hiding stuff. The thought process was what's done in the dark won't come to the light. It's a secret. Who will know? But as

I recap that phrase I believe it goes like this: "What's done in the dark will come to the light".

You might ask what has The Blue Room got to do with this book? Well, I love the way you ask questions. If walls could talk, they would tell you a thing or two. Keep looking and you'll find the answers. The Blue Room represents the family secrets behind closed doors. It epitomizes that old saying, "What happens in this house stays in this house." Some hidden things could be right in your face. You'll have to look more closely. It may be hiding behind a wall; or it might just be there on the wall, waiting to be explored. Watch, Look and Listen. It might be in that very picture or on that same wall that holds the picture.

The Blue Room – Geraldine's Room

You've heard the old saying: "a picture is worth a thousand words". There's a wall dying to tell you about what you are wondering about; and this time "Curiosity Won't Kill the Cat". It will simply enlighten you. Mere curiosity as found in this book will inspire you to want more. You may find yourself standing on "tip toe" in anticipation. The Blue Room will have you wondering about what comes next, and how do I get inside the room with the other readers.

Let's take a look and find out what's really going on.

The Blue Room – Geraldine's Room

SECTION ONE

BEFORE THE BLUE ROOM

Chapter 1 - Way Back When

The situation among African American families is complicated by our shameless history of slavery and racial prejudice. Native Africans, from whom much of our African American populace is descended, brought their own patterns of kinship from diverse cultural and tribal affiliations with them to this country. Some kinship structures were patrilineal *(Relating to, based on, or tracing ancestral descent through the paternal line)*; some were matrilineal *(based on or relating to tracing ancestral descent through the maternal line)*; a few were of double descent. All placed a primary value on extended family relationships. These kinships were disrupted systematically by the institution of slavery. Both adults and children were sold without regard to blood or marriage ties.

If you haven't already, I would challenge you to research your lineage for a reality check concerning the record of marriage. You will find that the institution of slavery did indeed bring shame upon us. The role of the African American man as husband and father was systematically denied. Families were willfully separated by selling members to different plantations. You know the stories. The African American family had no physical, psychological, social, or economic protection. Split families wouldn't know who was related to who.

Many times, premarital sex was born out of the circumstances. This is not to condone this behavior – it is for the purpose of clarification concerning the origin of these behavioral patterns. The institution of slavery brought about and defiled kinships. Children born into slavery were "out of wedlock" by virtue of the institution itself. They were informally adopted into symbolic families not limited by blood ties. This resilient response to the disruption of natural kinship is still practiced in economically depressed African American communities where widespread illegitimacy reflects "the lengthening shadow of slavery."

I find myself identifying with the ever-lengthening chains of bondage that linked us to a shameful past. Let the record show that my very own great grandfather known as "Captain Nelson" the blue-eyed Irishman, fathered my grandmother "Pearla" and her six siblings out of wedlock. In an act of atonement, he gave to my grandparents 200 acres of land as a wedding gift. To legalize the transaction, my grandfather paid $1.00 for the land. Of course, great grandfather "Nelson" was eventually put away in the Milledgeville Sanitarium for the insane. A white man taking a stand and owning up to his illegitimate black family had to be insane. In these reflections, I see God working in and through their circumstances with His sustaining power. That same staying power that has brought us through test after test.

Mitchell L. Lee, Sr, Pearl Bell Easton Lee, & two of their children

Grandpa & Grandma

Children at home in Eatonton

11 MARCH 1986

DEATHS OF THE LEE FAMILY MEMBERS

MITCHELL L. LEE, SR WAS BORN SEPTEMBER 15, 1876 AT LYNCHBURG, GEORGIA, NEAR EATONTON, GEORGIA. HE DIED SEPTEMBER 21 1954 IN DETROIT, MICHIGAN HE IS BURIED IN THE FAMILY CEMETARY IN EATONTON, GEORGIA.

PEARL BELL EASTON LEE WAS BORN APRIL 28, 1881 OUT FROM EATONTON, GEORGIA NEAR BETHEL CHURCH. SHE DIED JULY 30, 1942 IN THE HOME HOUSE IN EATONTON, GEORGIA. SHE IS BURIED NEXT TO HER HUSBAND IN THE FAMILY CEMETARY (REID) IN EATONTON, GEORGIA. TWO OF GRAND PAPA AND GRAND MAMA CHILDREN ARE ALSO BURIED HER - THEY DIED WHEN BABIES.

ESTELLE VIRGINIA LEE WILLIAMS LIVED IN MACON, GEORGIA BUT DIED IN ATLANTA, GEORGIA AT HER SISTER"S HOME.(IDELLA"S HOME). SHE DIED JULY 18, 1946. SHE IS BURIED IN MACON, GEORGIA IN THE WILLIAMS FAMILY CEMETARY.

JULIUS C. LEE BORN MAY 21, 1914. HE DIED DECEMBER 21, 1955 IN DETROIT, MICHIGAN. BURIED IN DETROIT MICHIGAN.

MITCHELL A. LEE, JR BORN AUGUST 8, 1908. HE DIED AUGUST 24, 1976 IN ATLANTA, GEORGIA. BURIED IN DETROIT, MICHIGAN

CLARENCE A. LEE BORN OCTOBER 27, 1916. HE DIED OCTOBER 7, 1985. BURIED IN DETROIT, MICHIGAN

WILLIW E. LEE DIED AT AGE SIX MONTHS.

GUY H. LEE DIED AT AGE NINE MONTHS.

MINNIE LEE, MITCHELL L. LEE"S SECOND WIFE WAS BURIED FEBRUARY 17, 1968 AT THE BROWN CHAPEL AME CHURCH IN EATONTON, GEORGIA. THAT WAS MITCHELL, HER HUSBAND"S CHURCH FOR MANY YEARS. MITCHELL TOOK HIS CHILDREN TO BROWN CHAPEL WHEN THEY WERE TINY TOTS. WHEN THEY BECAME TEEN AGERS, THEIR MOTHER, PEARL DEID, JOINED THE STANDFORVILLE AME CHURCH. THIS CHURCH WAS NEARER TO THE HOME AND THE CHILDREN JOINED HER AT STANDFORVILLE. HER FUNERAL WAS HELD HERE. PAPA"S, MITCHELL L, WAS HELD AT BROWN CHAPEL.

THE FAMILY OF MITCHELL L. LEE, SR AND PEARL BELL EASTON LEE   11 MARCH 1986

FRANK EDWARD LEE WAS BORN DECEMBER 31, 1900 IN EATONTON, GEORGIA (WILLARD). HE WAS NAMED FOR ONE OF HIS MOTHER"S BROTHER. HE LIVES IN EATONTON, GEROGIA.

MITCHELL A. LEE, JR WAS BORN AUGUST 8, 1908 IN EATONTON, GEORGIA. HE DIED AUGUST 24, 1976 IN ATLANTA, GEORGIA. HE CAME TO EATONTON, GEORGIA TO ATTEND HIS AUNT"S, MAUD ALFORD, FUNERAL. HE DIED AT HIS SISTER, IDELLA, HOME IN ATLANTA, GEORGIA. HE IS BURIED IN DETROIT, MICHIGAN, HE WAS NAMED FOR HIS FATHER.

JULIUS C. LEE WAS BORN MAY 21, 1914 IN EATONTON, GEORGIA. HE DIED DECEMBER 27, 1955 IN DETROIT, MICHIGAN. HE IS BURIED IN DETROIT. HE WAS NAMED FOR JULIUS CEASAR OF SHAKESPEARE.

CLARENCE A. LEE WAS BORN OCTOBER 27, 1916 IN EATONTON, GEORGIA HE DIED OCTOBER 7, 1985 IN DETROIT, MICHIGAN. HE IS BURIED IN DETROIT, MICHIGAN. HE WAS NAMED FOR HIS FATHER"S BROTHER.

JAMES M. LEE WAS BORN APRIL 24, 1924 IN EATONTON, GEROGIA. HE LIVES IN DETROIT, MICHIGAN WITH HIS FAMILY. HE WAS NAMED FOR HIS MOTHER"S BROTHER.

GUY M. LEE DIED AT AGE NINE MONTHS. HE WAS NAMED FOR ONE OF HER MOTHER'S UNCLES.

ESTELLE V. LEE WILLIAMS WAS BORN SEPTEMBER 20, 1901 IN EATONTON, GEORGIA. SHE DIED JULY 18, 1946. SHE DIED IN ATLANTA, GEORGIA AT IDELLA"S HOME. SHE IS BURIED IN MACON, GEORGIA. SHE WAS NAMED FOR HER MOTHER"S SISTER.

PATIENCE ORDELL LEE SINGLETON (IDELLA) (BAY) WAS BORN NOVEMBER 15, 1903 IN EATONTON, GEORGIA. SHE WAS NAMED FOR HER FATHER'S MOTHER. SHE LIVES IN ATLANTA, GEORGIA WITH HER FAMILY.

ROSA BEATRICE LEE GILLON WAS BORN MAY 19, 1911 IN EATONTON, GEORGIA. SHE WAS NAMED FOR HER MOTHER'S SISTER. SHE LIVES IN MILWAUKEE, WISCONSIN WITH HER FAMILY

ERMA LUCILE LEE DURLEY WAS BORN JANUARY 20, 1920 IN EATONTON, GEORGIA. SHE WAS NAMED FOR ONE OF HER MOTHER'S SISTERS

WILLIE EUGENE LEE DIED AT AGE SIX MONTHS. SHE WAS NAMED FOR ONE OF HER MOTHER'S BROTHERS.

Chapter 2 - The Cover Up

My mother was the youngest girl of eleven children raised on a 200-acre farm in the south. As the older children married and moved away, they helped by sending for the younger children. By this means all might have an opportunity to live a better lifestyle and get an education.

Home House - Eatonton, GA

Therefore, at an early age my mother was sent to live with her eldest sister's family in Macon, Georgia. This was a unique situation as they were the overseers of the Blind Academy there in Macon. This afforded Mom an opportunity to attend school and be raised in what was determined to be a better quality of life. She had what was considered to be the very best of opportunities for a woman of color. The fact that she lived with a sister and brother-in-law who were well off and established in the community improved her ability to move forward.

The color of her skin was also a factor that was vitally important in determining how far she could go. *You know: if you're white you're all right, if you're brown stick around, if you're black get back* (a cliché from back in the day).

Eventually, however, my mother would be sent onward to another sister's family in Atlanta to continue this upward trend. She was now able to move toward bettering her education and lifestyle. But this is where the story takes a turn.

Mom - Erma Lee

That train of thought was cut off when "life" happened to her. No one ever expected that Mom would get pregnant. Not once, but three times. I was third. Now I know that this was an act of God because the others did not survive.

Back in the day, the outhouse (Jon, or Out-Suite) was literally outdoors. "Slop jars," "tin tubs," "wash basins," "rub boards" and throwing the dish water out the back door was the lifestyle. There was no plumbing available, but there was an element of pride because they owned these possessions. If I sound sarcastic – well, the truth will set you free. It was called living off the land. Everyone had chores to do and learned from their experience. The formula for success was defined by these criteria.

If a young woman was with child, or as the Bible says: "with suck," she was a disgrace to the whole family. Therefore, she would simply be sent away to cover up the shame. The whole family participated in the cover up. As a result, she would be sent to live with a relative far away from prying eyes. The baby became the relative's child by simply blending in with the rest of the family.

Mom - Erma Lee

This practice was common among family members to bring the younger ones into their families to nurture and help shape their futures. It was not considered to be an imposition – it was just the way things were done. This is where my story comes in.

Chapter 3 – Trials and Tribulations

It was 1938. My mother was on a train bound from the south going north. She would eventually end up in Detroit, Michigan with her eldest brother and his family. Once again, she was taken in by the *"extended family"* to preserve and keep the family tied together. This action was taken so that she could escape the disgrace she would have had to endure had she remained in the south.

She lived in Atlanta with her older sister's family until the unthinkable happened. She became pregnant out of wedlock. There had been a "shot gun" wedding that went awry! The groom ran away and joined the army! That was not in the plan. It was unacceptable and not going to be tolerated.

In today's society, it has become quite acceptable to have children out of wedlock, and engagements last forever. Back in biblical days, however, engagements were long, the couples were put together by their parents, end of story. Life back in the day had many cover-ups going on. The truth be told there was a whole lot more going on behind the scenes than was evident. This is one of many scenarios or conclusions that may be drawn from within this story. At least it might appear that way. Same circumstances and strategies, utilizing different strokes for different folks. The bible tells us in the book of Ecclesiastes 1:9 *"The thing that hath been, it is that which shalt be; and that which is done is that which shall be done; and there is no new thing under the sun."* In other words, there is nothing new under the sun. Same motives with different methodology.

Getting back to the resolve of this dilemma, the matter was handled literally by forcing the perpetrators to marry. The child became part of a legal marriage, covering up the shame. They called it a "shotgun" wedding. It was like having a shot gun held to your head forcing a marriage made in hell. Now, way back in the day (biblical days that is); the woman would have been stoned to death.

To add insult to injury for Mom, her husband joined the army to escape the responsibility of a wife and child. She found herself abandoned, alone, and trapped in her circumstances with no way out, and no say so in the matter. Her depression along with the unbearable heat and being six months pregnant was undeniably horrific. Here she was six months into her pregnancy feeling hot and sickly. She perspired and longed for relief, for it to be over. She wanted to disappear as though she was having a bad dream. The thought and humility of it all sickened her even more. The problem was relocated and dealt with in a different environment among strangers in an effort to cover up the shame and hurt.

The train went clickety clack, clickety clack along the long hard and arduous tracks making its way up north. The young girl felt alone and betrayed. The long train ride was too much for her. When the train arrived, her brother was waiting at the depot after 24 miserable hours. She was weakened and exhausted. In humility, she proceeded to approach her brother to go with him to her new home; unknowingly, her baby would not survive and was "still born," relief or tragedy? The trip and circumstances surrounding the trip had been too much. The dramatics of this experience caused my mother to grieve. How was she going to receive this news driven by the good and the bad outcome? The impending news came upon arriving home.

The ride through the city was intimidating. It was so different from the rural place she grew up in. There were so few trees, more automobiles, sidewalks, people, and buildings. How was she going to adjust to this new environment? It was overwhelming!

Somehow, she would have to make the adjustment because there was no turning back. After the long ride through the city, they drove into a neighborhood of very large houses. There were children playing on the sidewalks and drunks on the street corner near a small Mom & pop grocery store. This was very different from gleaning from the farms where she grew up.

Mitchell Lee Jr.

There were no "outhouses." There was "indoor" plumbing. She thought to herself, "they must be rich." There were cars parked in front of every house, indeed they must be rich! If she only knew that this neighborhood, would become the "hood."

Although this eradicated the physical visibility of her condition, it did not remove the pain that comes with the shame. Instead, it added to the hidden secrets already filling her inner sanctum with more grief to carry and bury.

The north had become a melting pot for shaping and molding the many families sent away to become successful. However, there were those who came under a very different set of circumstances. Circumstances that were created by hidden and deeply rooted guilt and shame.

The men were the bread winners and brought home the bacon. It was called living "high-on-the-hog"! Upward mobility came in many forms. You see, being taken in by the *"extended family"* was to preserve and keep the family tied together from a distance.

James Lee, Mitchell Lee & friend

Now we all know that being sent away from home in those days was not always relative to upward mobility. Many times, there were secrets being covered up. The problem was relocated and dealt with in a different environment among strangers to cover up the shame and hurt.

So then, the *"family"* sacrificed much and gave even more of themselves, constituted out of pride and shame. Once you are a part of the melting pot, you simply blend in with everyone else so that no one can pen-point your exact situation. Even if deep down they know the truth they are part of the meltdown sworn to secrecy. It was considered better for them to take it to their grave first, never telling a soul.

Well, you would think this would be the end of this story. However, it only becomes more intense. I was born a couple of years later in Detroit. I guess you're wondering how I happened on the scene with the man of the house being away in the war.

Well, you know we look for love in all the wrong places; well, isn't that what any wounded person would do? Mom was no different. She met and dated the man who was to become my biological father. Mom met this young man; they fell in love and made a baby girl. That would be me. Well guess what? She's still married to the man who ran away to the army and abandoned her. The guilt and shame of pregnancy results in her making the decision to dissolve her relationship with my biological father. Once again, the secrets continue, and the knowledge of this vital person in my life was kept from me. Remember there was no DNA testing. You would think this would be the end of this story; however, life goes on.

In some way she feels an obligation to a marriage that is valid in name only. When she found out she was pregnant yet again, she again began to feel guilty and ashamed. These emotions were based on past indiscretions that were engrained in her due to past mistakes and generational curses. Now, she is feeling guilty for having cheated on a husband who never acknowledged her as his wife (go figure).

Due to IIS (Ignorance, Insecurity and Shame), she makes yet another decision to cover up, by electing to have the child and sending her lover away. Somehow, she feels an obligation to a marriage that is invalid because it's in name only – made up to cover up.

Within a short period of time, along came me. In Detroit, I was born in what was known at the time as the east side "black bottom." After the birth of yours truly, and the agony of feeling defeated, Mom decides to get a new start with her sister's family who lived even further north with very cold winters. I guess it's becoming clear by now that this has become a lifestyle and a way of escape. Mom makes a new start.

At age three, my mother and I moved to Milwaukee, WI to yet another sister's family while my adopted father served in the War. The draft was implemented and imposed. Men are separated from their families. The women go to work in the factories. The family is split apart by the experience of War. In Milwaukee Mom was able to get work in a factory where military weapons were produced. Most of the men were away at war, so women worked in the factories making weapons for the warfare.

After the war ended, we returned to Detroit where Mom reconciled with her husband. We became the *"traditional family unit"* with the husband, wife, and child. My father being the "breadwinner" and my mother the "homemaker." No, we did not have a station wagon or a dog, but we did have a large family car, and there was only one child, me. We don't escape the obligations of the *"extended family"* because inevitably this way of life enabled my family to send for my mother's youngest brother who was the last to leave the nest. By now we had become the *"extended family."* This cycle completes its circle to reconnect with my grandparents who ultimately will be brought to live with us and be nurtured in their golden years.

The interaction I experienced with my aunts, uncles, and cousins gave me a sense of family unity and security. We were a close-knit family and have remained so throughout the years.

Chapter 4 – A Time of Reckoning

Ironically, when the war ended, Mom's husband came home to join us in Milwaukee. To everyone's amazement, he had gotten in touch with reality and wanted to make amends. He made up for everything by legally adopting me. Everyone knew but me.

Flesh and blood did not reveal to me the information I'm about to share with you. The unction of the Holy Spirit came upon me, leading me to ask Mom if the man that we were living with was really my father? At the age of 18 God gives me revelation. I had believed for all those years that he was my biological father who had come home from the war. Never questioned it. I did not have a clue that he wasn't my biological father. I had been told that my father was in the war. I had been led to believe that he would return some day. Remember, that was part of the facade. Everyone knew but me. I had given the word oblivious a new level of being in denial!

The union was reconciled and all

Mom & Dad – Erma L. & Grady B. Burley

forgiven. I was officially adopted. However, there was yet another cover up. It was agreed that I was never to know that I had been adopted. I never knew who my biological father was. The secret was hidden right under my nose amongst relatives who knew the truth. No mention was ever made to me by any of them.

I received final confirmation of this truth upon applying for my birth certificate. My real father's name had been crossed out and replaced with the name of my mother's husband. Once again, there was another form of deception to cover up, while yet another lie surfaces. God works in mysterious ways, as you will find out. Keep on reading.

Shortly after my adopted father returned, we went back to Detroit to live. That was an interesting part of the journey. We lived from place to place, mostly in one-room boarding houses. Many times, we would live in one-bedroom. Mom and Dad slept in a bed together. I slept on a cot at the foot of the bed. My bed companions were bedbugs. We had bathroom and kitchen

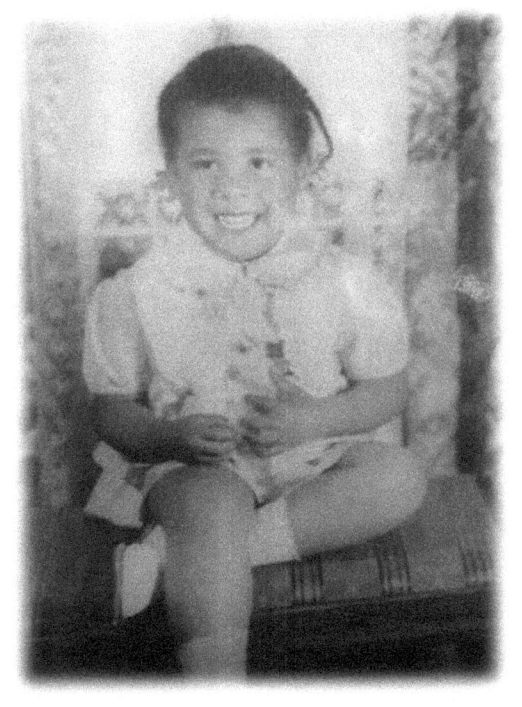

Geraldine Lee Burley

privileges that were shared with other tenants who had adjoining rooms.

This was called "room and board." In addition to our neighbors, we also had the company of rats and roaches throughout the house. But overall, we learned to live in these circumstances. The fun part of all of this was when Dad would fumigate the house. We would have to leave the house in the evening to allow enough time to air it out from the deadly fumes coming from the chemicals that were used. We would go to the neighborhood theatre for the midnight show and watch movies until we could return home. All that mattered was that we were together.

SECTION TWO

THE BLUE ROOM

Chapter 5 – His Plan, His Purpose

Returning to Detroit with my mother and the man I believed to be my father turned out to be a blessing. I was experiencing life from another perspective. Moving around from place to place and not settling down right away threw me into a mode of challenges I would have to meet. I was exposed to all kinds of people, not knowing there were the good and the bad to consider.

Ways were being made out of no way. I was sheltered and uninformed about the challenges we all faced. After all, I was just a kid being a kid. My parents were trying to give me a new perspective on life without all the ups and downs that my mother had faced alone. She was determined that I would not have to go through the trials and tribulations as she did.

After much to do with coming together as a family, Dad finally found us a permanent home on the West side of Detroit, which at the time was an all-white community. Yes, we were among the first black folk to live on the block. I had heard the grown folk talking about "Jim Crow" thinking that we had left all that behind us in the South, that this would be a different experience.

The neighborhood was beautiful. The grass was green. The trees were tall forming an ark down the middle of the street. The houses were well kept, and in a short time the neighborhood was transformed into a community of black folk. Of course, as the blacks moved in, the white folk moved out, running away from the color of our skin. Yet, I was clueless, not having any idea that the spirit of Jim Crow had infiltrated the neighborhood surrounding us with its prejudices.

Before moving into this neighborhood, Dad contracted to purchase a home in another community called Conant Gardens. Because of segregation and discrimination that had expanded to the north, I would hear innuendoes, but I was still a child being sheltered. Therefore, I had no idea of what all that meant. So, whatever was done in the dark was blocked from the light, leaving me oblivious to reality. Therefore, I was spared a good deal of direct hits from the "enemy." They would come later after experiencing life for myself, when things began to come to light, and I began to mature.

Later on, we found that the best opportunities were to follow through on intuition and dreams. Back in the day, job opportunities were with the automobile industry, or the steel mills, where most black folk moving from the south to the north would end up working. Eventually Dad got a job at the steel mill. and after much determination, struggle, and sacrifice, he was able to purchase a home.

Family – Me, Mom, Uncles & Cousins - 1958

The economics of that era dictated the family lifestyle.

For example:

> ⇒ Decline in prosperity brought families together out of necessity – there was only one bathroom and 1 or 2 shared bedrooms.
>
> ⇒ It was common practice for the men to help one another in obtaining jobs in the same factory. Such was the case with my father, uncles and eventually my husband. As prosperity increased, the family unit was split apart. With the ability to have 2 bathrooms and separate bedrooms for each child, the attitude of sharing diminished.
>
> ⇒ Traditionally, the local church played an important role in the family unit. The history of the church was in each of the local churches within the community. We revolved and evolved from one another – different denominations, yet Christ centered.
>
> ⇒ The family ate their meals together at the same table. The elders prayed and grace was always given before every meal. The rules were:
>   - -meals were served in the dining room or at the kitchen table, period.
>   - -you ate what was put before you, period.
>   - -there was no singing at the table, period.

- -chores had to be done before any form of entertainment was undertaken, period.
- -homework was done, period.
- -permission was asked and/or given for the privilege of doing just about anything and everything, period.
- -nothing was taken for granted, period.
- -children were seen and not heard, period.

Period means, no questions, no debates, no negotiation – just DO IT, period!

Our Home in Detroit, MI

Warranty Deed – *Our home in Detroit, MI*

Chapter 6 – Saved from Stardom

Now, back then children formed strong bonds and created their own entertainment, because entertainment options weren't easily obtained. The television had just been invented, and we couldn't afford one. Our parents only made enough money to make ends meet. Television was not a necessity, and only what was needed was purchased. So, for entertainment, the children took their activities outside which pretty much took place in the alley; on the sidewalks, or in the streets; we even created our own games to play outside. The younger children had to be inside when the streetlights came on, or else you got the "beat down."

Geraldine L. Burley

I am reminded of the time when I didn't obey the command to be in the house before the streetlights came on. I waited for my next-door neighbor friend who had gone inside, to come back and play with me. While I waited, I was approached by a stranger on my front porch. He asked me to give him a look at my crack. Being small and vulnerable at age 5, I didn't understand his request. I showed him a crack in the railing of the porch. He said if I showed him, he would give me a dime.

At that very moment, deliverance sprung forth, as my mother called out my name loudly, "GET IN THIS HOUSE NOW!" The predator ran to his car and sped away in his car.

Now here's where the story takes a turn of events. As we became teenagers we were allowed to go to movies or to the skating rink with our friends, but we had curfews to adhere to. Spending evenings singing on the street corners is what we enjoyed most. It seemed like everyone loved singing. I guess you've heard all this before from the baby boomer crowd, but I want to share with you how my girlfriends and I almost became super stars. Destiny was delayed in the form of our becoming "super stars," but for me, it was not denied in terms of destiny. What I found out is that destiny is not always defined by how we perceive it. When opportunity comes knocking at your door you are not always ready for what comes with it.

Gloria McKenney & Geraldine L. Burley

Ladies' Club – Geraldine and friends

Nearly every evening after school, when the homework and chores were done, me, and three of my girlfriends would get together at each other's house in our bedrooms. Coincidentally our bedrooms were upstairs and painted blue, so, we called them the "blue rooms." That's where we shared all our hopes, dreams, and secrets. We laughed, cried, and sang together. Our code was, "Let's meet in the blue room." It is from that experience I find myself writing this book entitled "The Blue Room". I find myself reflecting on many years before and years after. I believe the Lord intervened on our behalf, probably keeping us out of trouble and on His path of mercy and grace.

We were sixteen and typical teenagers full of hopes and dreams. One day while we were browsing through the Michigan Chronicle (a local newspaper) there appeared an ad soliciting four female vocalists to do background singing for a newly formed company called KUDO Recording Company. You guessed it, we answered the ad. The studio was in the basement of one of the founders and producers. His name was Bobby Hamilton. We auditioned and were hired immediately. We had no clue how close we were to fame and fortune. We were right there. We would practice religiously at home, in the studio, in the car, on the street corner, on the way to and from school. I would dream about the music every night. I couldn't get it out of my head. It was all we could think about!

It was there that we met Holland Dozier & Holland and other up and coming artists. At times, we sang background for them. We also met the very popular singing group called "The Falcons" with whom we became good friends. We sang background for them as well. As I recall, Smokey Robinson and "the Miracles," other musicians and songwriters i.e., Hamilton Bohannon, Bobbie Hamilton, and others had just come on the scene as well.

Singing Group – Joe Stubbs & The Falcons - 1958

One day we received an invitation to audition for Berry Gordy, who at the time, was unbeknownst to us was a part of KUDO Recording Company. He was looking for four young ladies to become the "Supremes." You heard me! YES, I said the "SUPREMES"! The audition took place at the home of Mr. Berry Gordy's sister who at that time lived on Buena Vista Street in Detroit. We fit the profile of what Mr. Gordy was looking for in his vision. Of course, we were clueless about the significance of the clarion call that had come to us. Well, lo and behold, we passed our audition and there we were without any competition.

The contract had been drawn up and all we had to do was to have our parents sign off on it... But sadly, things were not so simplistic. WAIT A MINUTE, here's where we missed the boat. We weren't even worried that this would be a problem. We never considered such a thing, leaning to our own understanding or imagination. But lo, divine intervention came in the form of another stratospheric nature that would override our call to become super stars better known as the Supremes, because of a "Clarion Call" that had been established in the corridors of heaven.

This was not to be our season of fame and fortune. We had been designated for another season, yet to come. All we knew was that we were on our way. Sadly, the story was not so simple. Just as suddenly as we received the news, bad news followed.

Geraldine Lee Burley

When we approached our parents about what happened, they expressed some pride in our accomplishment. Yet, they were not about to give their permission for us to become super stars at the expense of completing our education. Nothing could come before our education. So that was the end of that!

Just as quickly as fame and fortune had come, it was gone. There was no way our parents were going to allow us to be exposed to a life of alcohol, drugs, and fast living. You know, we were good girls who had been designated by our parents to become educated, married, have babies, and increase the world's population. But we were to do it in the tradition of making an honest living because we had been raised right! No devil in hell was going to get his hands on us. Little did we know or understand that God had another plan and purpose for us. It was not shaking our bustiest and booties or tail-feathers, or having money thrown at us. Not now, not ever.

Later, I met a man during my brief attempt to enter college and he invited me to have lunch with him. He seemed sophisticated and intelligent. Therefore, now looking for a fresh start, and without hesitation, I accepted the invitation. I was to come to his house where he lived with his parents, so he said, and I thought nothing of it.

Out on the date with my new friend, it was agreed upon that we would get together at his house for lunch. Once again, I had been set up without knowing what I had gotten myself into, by accepting this invitation. This is what will happen some of the time when the facts are kept from you, and you don't have a clue. There is no mention of the consequences that may result from your own indiscretions.

The Lord began to speak loudly to me, but I didn't know HIS VOICE. While waiting for the lunch to be served, I heard a "Still Small Voice" in my ear, calling my name saying: YOU ARE SPECIAL, AND I HAVE SET YOU APART. I looked around to see where the voice was coming from. At first, I thought I was hearing things. I didn't see anyone there, so making small talk, I proceeded to ask my date the question, do you sometimes think you are special to God? He probably thought I was just making conversation. However, I had been set up to get up and get out of there, and I never thought about where this was going.

God came with divine intervention to keep me from falling for the "Okey-doke" but I remained clueless. God had whispered in my ear with a Clarion Call (resounding and clear). The real call on my life came loud and clear at age 17. Unfortunately, it wasn't clear to me. I had been so sheltered about the "so called" facts of life that I just thought that everything was "hunky dory". I was walking into the arms of the enemy; but what the enemy meant for evil, God meant it for good.

Not knowing that I was being served up for lunch, the devil appeared to me as an angel of light, and I was overcome by the spirit of lust. My date had other plans, and I was to be his lunch. Easily and willingly, I dropped my guard, what little I had and did the unthinkable. In my mother's words – *"Keep you skirt on and your panties up."* I heard her voice but couldn't distinguish that it was God's voice from within her that I should have been listening for.

The spirit of seduction and rebellion crept in. I heard my mother warning me about what to do. But not knowing how to do it, I didn't adhere to it. What I didn't realize is that God was intervening from within me also, [*"Greater is he that is in me than he who is in the world"*] to prevent me from crossing the line, but it had been too late. Furthermore, I didn't realize that God was trying to get my attention, because my mind was on sin and worldly things. So, before I knew it, I was standing in the "Blue Room" with *the lust of the flesh, and the pride of life* establishing another secret. Oh' "If Walls Could Talk." I had been "*duped*" into relinquishing my virginity to a man I had just met. If the enemy can't get you one way, he'll try another. Of course, that relationship didn't last long after that; but God.

Recording Agreement – Kudo Recording Associates

NAME OF ARTIST: *Quadello* RECORDING AGREEMENT   DATE OF EXECUTION

KUDO RECORDING ASSOCIATION   4-1-1958

ADDRESS: Busby - 5374 Allendale
Cortez - 6288 Seubaldt
Barnette - 6393 Colfax

We hereby employ you for the purpose of making phonograph records.

1. You do hereby agree to record solely and exclusively for KUDO RECORDING ASSOCIATION, in accordance with the provisions of this agreement. It is agreed that you will record a minimum of __8__ phonograph sides, with additional sides to be recorded at KUDO'S election. In the event that more than the minimum number of sides are recorded during any year in which this agreement is in effect, KUDO shall have the option of applying the excess sides recorded in any one (1) year towards the requirements for subsequent year or years.

2. Royalties due under this agreement will be computed upon the basis of __3%__ percent of ninety (90%) percent of the retail selling price, exclusive of Federal Excise Tax and less the retail cost of album covers, of all records sold in the United States and Canada, embodying performances hereunder on both sides thereof, and one-half (½) the amount of such royalty for ninety (90%) percent of the retail selling price, exclusive of Federal Excise Tax, and less the retail cost of album covers, of all records sold in the United States and Canada embodying performances hereunder on only one (1) side thereof, and, in the event long-play records are sold in the United States and Canada embodying performances hereunder, which performances are less than the musical content on one side thereof, the royalty paid hereunder shall be in the same proportion to ninety (90%) percent of the retail selling price, exclusive of Federal Excise Tax, and less the retail cost of album covers, of all such records sold in the United States and Canada, as the performance hereunder bears to the entire musical content of said records. For all records sold hereunder outside of the United States and Canada, the royalties therefor shall be one-half (½) of the royalty rates above set forth. For all records sold hereunder outside of the United States, either by KUDO or any of its licensees, KUDO may, from time to time, at its sole election, base their percentages either upon the retail list prices in the country of sale, the country of manufacture, or the retail list prices of England. Royalties aforesaid for all records sold outside of the United States are to be computed in the national currency of the the country where the retail prices above listed apply and are to be paid only when such royalties are received by KUDO in the United States, and in the dollar equivalent at the rate of exchange at the time KUDO receives payment. The royalty due on account of the sale of any record produced hereunder shall be at the rate of the royalty in effect hereunder at the time of the recording session for said record. KUDO will make a non-returnable advance to the Artist of Aftra scale for each side recorded hereunder, payable within fourteen days after each recording session.

3. It is agreed that the services of the Artist are unique and extraordinary. Therefore, the Artist agrees that during the term of this contract he will not perform any material for any person other than KUDO RECORDING COMPANY, for reproduction of any kind of his performances

-more-

2/Kudo Agreement

or any part thereof, and that for five years after the expiration date of this contract, or any extension or any renewal thereof, the ARTIST will not perform any material recorded hereunder for any person, other than KUDO RECORDING ASSOCIATION, (otherwise known as "Company") for the purpose of making phonograph records or any reproductions of any kind of the performances by any method now or hereafter known.

4. All recordings, records and reproductions made therefrom, together with the performances embodied therein, shall be and remain entirely the property of KUDO RECORDING ASSOCIATION, free of any claim by the ARTIST or any person deriving any rights or interest from the ARTIST. In addition, KUDO RECORDING ASSOCIATION shall have the right to make records or other reproductions of the performances embodied in such recordings by any method now or hereafter known, and to sell and deal in the same under any trade-marks or trade-names, or labels designated by KUDO RECORDING ASSOCIATION, or KUDO RECORDING ASSOCIATION may, at its own election, refrain therefrom.

5. KUDO RECORDING ASSOCIATION is granted the right to use and to allow others to use the name and likenesses of the ARTIST and biographical matter concerning the ARTIST for advertising, trade purposes, and otherwise, without restriction in connection with phonograph records made persuant to this contract. KUDO will not use or authorize any direct endorsement of any record or performances without prior written consent of the ARTIST.

6. KUDO agrees that it will advance the necessary cost of orchestral accompaniment and arrangements; these items to be treated as an advance against such royalties as may become due in accordance with this agreement. An accounting is to be made of royalties due, and the net amounts will be paid within forty-five (45) days after June 30th and December 31st of each year during which records made hereunder are sold.

7. The Artist warrants and agrees that no prior contract or agreement of any kind entered into by the Artist, or any prior performance by the Artist, will interfere in any manner with complete performance of the within agreement by both parties hereto.

8. KUDO shall have the right to call upon the Artist to repeat to a reasonable extent any work without further payment until a satisfactory master recording has in the opinion of the company been made.

9. KUDO shall have the right to give, lend, lease or sell to any person, firm or company, matrices, stampers or master recordings from which records reproducing all or any of the Artist's services hereunder may be manufactured or sold, and shall have the right to grant permission to any such person, firm or company to use such matrices, stampers or master recordings to manufacture and sell records therefrom.

10. In the event of the Artist by illness or absence or any other cause, not being able to fulfill the provisions herein to the reasonable satisfaction of KUDO, then KUDO shall have the option to terminate this agreement forthwith.

11. If the fulfilling of this agreement shall become impossible

--more--

3/Kudo Agreement

by reason of "force Majeure" or any other cause outside the control of the parties hereto, then either party shall be entitled (by giving notice in writing to the other party hereto and without incurring any liability for damages or compensation) to suspend the operation of this agreement until such time as such fulfillment shall again become possible provided always that if the operation of the agreement shall be suspended as aforesaid, then KUDO shall during the period of such suspension continue to pay to the artist the royalties due to him or her under this agreement so long as any such royalties shall be payable by reason of the manufacture and sale of records under the provisions of this agreement. In the event that this agreement has become suspended, as provided for in this paragraph, the term of this agreement shall be extended for a period equivalent to the period of such suspension, providing that fulfillment of said agreement again becomes possible. Artist does further agree that in the event that this agreement shall become suspended, in accordance with the provisions of this paragraph, that said Artist will not, during the period that said contract may be so suspended, record for any other person, firm or corporation, for the purpose of making phonograph records. In the event that any monthly or other advances are required to be made by KUDO to the Artists, in accordance with the provisions of the agreement, KUDO will be excused from making payment of said advances during any period that this agreement may become suspended in accordance with the provisions of this agreement.

12. The services to be performed by the Artist herein means the performance by Artist of literary or musical works under any method now or hereafter known whereby the performance of the Artist is reproduced. Performance hereunder includes singing, speaking or playing an instrument, alone or with others, and also includes conducting. "Artist" means the party or parties hereby contracting with KUDO, whether male or female, singular or plural.

13. In the event that any recordings made hereunder are participated in by any other Artists who are then under exclusive recording agreements with KUDO, the royalties due hereunder, for said recordings, shall be the royalties above provided for divided by the number of Artists participating therein, including artist herein.

14. If KUDO does not record the agreed minimum number of sides, KUDO'S liability shall be limited to the agreed non-returnable advance for all unrecorded sides.

15. The individual or individuals signing this contract, known professionally as _Quadello_, do hereby warrant to KUDO that he, or she, or they, is/are the lawful owners of the right to use the name _Quadello_ in connection with their performance thereunder and hereunder, and that no other persons have any right or claim in or to said name, and do hereby grant to KUDO full and complete right to the use of said name in connection with phonograph records to be reproduced and sold in accordance herewith. The Artists herein do further warrant that they are the owners of the copyright issued in connection with the name.

16. The period of this contract shall be for _2 yrs_ commencing with the date hereof.

-more-

4/Kudo Agreement

17. Royalties for all albums sold embodying performances hereunder shall be one-half ($\frac{1}{2}$) of the above royalty rates, except that in no case shall royalties for the sale of albums be less than two and one-half (2-$\frac{1}{2}$) percent of ninety (90%) percent.

18. KUDO is hereby granted five (5) several options of extending this agreement for five (5) separate terms of one (1) year each. Each and all of said options may be excercised by KUDO by means of written notice sent to the Artist, at the address hereinafter set forth, by registered mail, at least thirty days prior to any expiration date, except that the notice of the excercise of the option for the first option year shall be sent to the Artist within thirty (30) days after the release of the last side to be recorded hereunder. In the event said options are excercised, this contract shall be deemed extended for the additional period of said options with all terms and conditions above set forth, except that the royalty rates, and the minimum number of sides to be recorded, during each of said option years, shall be as follows:

    1st option year - 8 sides - 2-$\frac{1}{2}$% of 90% - AFTRA scale
    2nd option year - 8 sides - 2-$\frac{1}{2}$% of 90% - AFTRA scale
    3rd option year - 8 sides - 3% of 90% - AFTRA scale
    4th option year - 8 sides - 3-$\frac{1}{2}$% of 90% - AFTRA scale
    5th option year - 8 sides - 4% of 90% - AFTRA scale

19. During the time provided herein for which KUDO shall have the option to exercise the first option, Artist does hereby agree that he will not record for any other person, firm or corporation.

20. For all purposes hereunder, the addresses of the parties hereto shall be as follows:

(Company)
KUDO RECORDING ASSOCIATION
1114 United Artists Building
Detroit 26, Mich. WO.2-7480

(Artists)

IN WITNESS WHEREOF the parties hereto have affixed their hands and seals the day and year first above written.

KUDO RECORDING ASSOCIATION
BY _Robert West_

_____ (SEAL)
_____ (SEAL)
_____ (SEAL)
_____ (SEAL)
_____ (SEAL)
_____ (SEAL)

_____ (WITNESS)

-oOo-

Popular Songwriter's Contract

AGREEMENT entered into this 17 day of 5-1958
by and between JANE WEST - HIGGINS MUSIC PUBLISHERS
1114 UNITED ARTISTS BUILDING, hereinafter designated as the PUBLISHER,
and Ernest L Burley, author and/or composer,
hereinafter jointly designated as the COMPOSER/480

WITNESSETH:

1. The COMPOSER hereby sells, assigns, transfers and delivers to the PUBLISHER, its successors and assigns, the original musical composition written and composed by Erma L Burley, at present entitled Sick Spell, which title may be changed by the PUBLISHER; including the title, words and music thereof, and all rights therein; and all copyrights and the rights to secure copyrights and any extensions and renewals of copyrights in the same and in any arrangements and adaptations thereof, throughout the world; and any and all other rights that the COMPOSER now has or to which he may be entitled or that he hereafter could or might secure with respect to this composition, if these presents had not been made, throughout the world; and to have and to hold the same absolutely unto the PUBLISHER its successors and assigns.

2. The COMPOSER hereby covenants, represents and warrants that the composition hereby sold is an original work and that neither said work nor any part thereof infringes upon the title or the literary or musical property or the copyright in any other work, and that he is the sole writer and composer and the sole owner thereof and of all the rights therein, and has not sold, assigned, set over, transferred, hypothecated or mortgaged any right, title or interest in or to the said composition or any part thereof, or any of the rights herein conveyed, and that he has not made or entered into any contract or contracts with any other person, firm or corporation whomsoever, affecting said composition or any right, title or interest therein, or in the copyright thereof, and that no person, firm or corporation other than the COMPOSER has or has had claims, or has claimed any right, title or interest in or to said work or any part thereof or any use thereof or of any copyright therein, and that said work has never been published, and that the COMPOSER has full right, power and authority to make this present instrument of sale and transfer.

3. In consideration of this agreement, the PUBLISHER agrees to pay the COMPOSER as follows:

    (a) An advance of $1.00 in hand paid, receipt of which is hereby acknowledged; or any other sum heretofore or hereafter advanced to the COMPOSER, which total sums shall be deductible from any payments hereafter becoming due to the COMPOSER under this agreement.

    (b) A royalty of .03 cents per copy on all regular piano copies sold and paid for in the United States of America.

    (c) A royalty of .03 cents per copy on any form of orchestration thereof sold and paid for in the United States of America.

    (d) A royalty of 10 for each use of the lyrics and music together, in any song book, song sheet, folio or similar publication containing at least five musical compositions.

    (e) For purposes of royalty statements, if a composition is printed and published in the United States, as to copies and rights sold in the Dominion of Canada, revenue therefrom shall be considered as of domestic origin. If, however, the composition is printed by a party other than the PUBLISHER in the Dominion of Canada, revenue therefrom shall be considered as originating in a foreign country.

    (f) An amount equal to 50 of all net receipts of the PUBLISHER in respect of any license issued authorizing the manufacture of the parts of instruments serving to mechanically reproduce the said composition, or to use the said composition in synchronization with sound motion pictures, or to reproduce it upon so called "electrical transcriptions" for broadcasting purposes; and of any and all net receipts of the PUBLISHER from any other source or right now known or which may hereafter come into existence.

    (g) A royalty of 50% of all net sums received by the PUBLISHER on regular piano copies and/or orchestrations thereof, and for the use of said composition in any folio or composite work, sold and paid for in any foreign country.

    (h) In the event that the said composition shall not now have lyrics, and lyrics are added to the said composition, the above royalties shall be divided equally between the COMPOSER and the other writers and composers.

4. It is specifically understood and agreed that the intention of this agreement is not, and the COMPOSER shall not be entitled to receive any part of the monies received by the PUBLISHER from the American Society of Composers, Authors and Publishers, or any other licensing agency from which the PUBLISHER may receive payments for the use of said musical composition in all countries of the world.

5. It is agreed that no royalties are to be paid for professional copies, copies disposed of as new issues, copies distributed for advertising purposes, or lyrics or music separately printed in any folio, book, newspaper, song sheet, lyric folio or magazine, or any other periodical, except as above set forth. It is also distinctly understood that no royalties are payable on consigned copies unless paid for, and not until such time as an accounting therefor can properly be made.

6. The PUBLISHER agrees that it will render to the COMPOSER, semi-annually on or about the 15th days of February and August of each year, a statement showing all sales and royalties earned by the said COMPOSER to the preceding December 31st and June 30th and will pay to him at the same time all royalties then due and owing.

7. The COMPOSER hereby expressly grants and conveys to the PUBLISHER the copyright of the aforesaid composition, with renewals, and with the right to copyright and renew the same, and the right to secure all copyrights and renewals of copyright and any and all rights therein that the COMPOSER may at any time be entitled to, and agrees to sign any and all other papers which may be required to effectuate this agreement. And the COMPOSER does hereby irrevocably authorize and appoint the PUBLISHER, its successors or assigns, his attorneys and representatives in their name or in his name to take and do such actions, deeds and things and make, sign, execute, acknowledge and deliver all such documents as may from time to time be necessary to secure the renewals and extensions of the copyright in the aforesaid composition, and to assign to the PUBLISHER, its successors and assigns, said renewal copyrights and all rights therein for the term of such renewals and extensions and the COMPOSER agrees upon the expiration of the first term of any copyright in the aforesaid composition in this or in any contract, to do, make, execute, acknowledge and deliver, or to procure the due execution, acknowledgment and delivery to the PUBLISHER, of all papers necessary in order to secure to it the renewals and extension of all copyrights in said compositions and all rights therein for the terms of such renewals and extensions.

8. The PUBLISHER agrees to publish the said musical composition in saleable form within one year after the receipt of lead sheet of the said composition. Should it fail to do so, the COMPOSER shall have the right, in writing, by registered mail, to demand the return of such unpublished composition, whereupon the PUBLISHER must within sixty days after receipt of such notice either publish the said composition, in which event this agreement shall remain in full force and effect, or upon failure so to publish, all rights of any and every nature granted to the PUBLISHER herein in connection with the said unpublished composition shall revert to and become the property of the COMPOSER and shall be reassigned to him.

In connection with the foregoing it is distinctly understood and agreed that if the PUBLISHER shall secure a commercial phonograph recording, or an electrical transcription, or a synchronization in a motion picture, the PUBLISHER; such recording, transcription or synchronization shall, for the purposes of this agreement, be deemed publication by the PUBLISHER.

9. The COMPOSER agrees that he will not transfer nor assign this agreement nor any interest therein nor any sums that may be or become due hereunder without the written consent of the PUBLISHER first hereon endorsed, and no purported assignment or transfer in violation of this restriction shall be valid to pass any interest to the assignee or transferee.

12. All questions and differences whatsoever which may at any time hereafter arise between the parties hereto touching these presents or the subject matter thereof, or arising out of or in relation thereto, and whether as to construction or otherwise, shall be referred to arbitration under the provisions and the supervision of the American Arbitration Association.

13. This agreement contains the entire understanding between the parties, and all of its terms, conditions and covenants shall be binding upon and shall inure to the benefit of the respective parties and their heirs, successors and assigns. No modification or waiver hereunder shall be valid unless the same is in writing and is signed by the parties hereto.

14. *Share*
Erma L Burley
Janet Carter
Geraldine Burley
Carol Carter
Sandra Burnette

IN WITNESS WHEREOF, the parties hereto have executed this agreement the day and year first above written.

14-5-1958

Robert West

Mitchell & Co.
Witness

By LANE - WEST - HIGGINS

Mary C Robinson
Witness

Composer Erma L Burley
           Geraldine Burley
Address   5374 Allendale

_____
Witness

Composer Sandra Burnette
Address   6390 Gulfox

_____
Witness

Composer Janet Carter
          Carol Carter
Address   5388 Seebaldt

Chapter 7 – The School of Hard Knocks

O' yes, we finished high school, even entered college. Ironically, the life they were saving us from found its way to us despite their strongest efforts. History repeated itself when I got pregnant and had to drop out of college. We finished high school, but none of us finished college. I got pregnant and married. They eventually got married too. We all had children. Ironically, life happened to us all over again. What was supposed to save us found its way back to us. We all ended up in the school of "hard knocks."

I believed in the institution of marriage, not in the real sense, but in the fairy-tale sense. I was taught that you get an education meaning a "high school diploma;" you get married, have children, and live happily ever after. End of Story.

I had to drop out of college and get married. Three children later and 15 years of anguish and mental abuse, I found myself on yet another journey. Life has a way of turning your tragedy into your salvation. I had three wonderful children born out of sexual and substance abuse. I lived in a dreaded marriage deeply rooted in denial because I was told that you must make the best of a bad situation (you know -- "for better or for worse") for the sake of the children. Not one single person outside of the family had a clue there was anything less than a perfect marriage going on. The cover up had surfaced again. It was the natural thing to do. The same kind of deception and denial I spoke of earlier, those closet skeletons that will keep you in bondage found their way back into our lives.

Somehow, despite all the negativity, I still believed in the institution of marriage, a bond not to be broken. The difference for me now is in the knowledge of the truth of Christ Jesus in my life and having that vertical connection with God. I have found that ignorance will kill you. *(My people are destroyed for a lack of knowledge. Hosea 4:6)* Thank God, that I serve a God of second chances. A long-suffering God, who despite all our wickedness and short comings, turns the negatives into positives; ordinary into the extraordinary.

I was an only child, sheltered and oblivious to life. I did not know that as perfect as the circumstances of my life appeared to be, dysfunctional spirits would in time rear their ugly heads. All is not what it appears to be because of those skeletons (secrets) lurking in the closet of your mind. Those same generational curses that we deny in our attempt to cover up any appearance of evil are still lurking around. Closet secrets will surface from out of the depth of a dark and ugly past. Holding on to secrets are the symptoms of a disease that leads to dementia. You see, my mother carried the bulk of her secret indiscretions to the grave in the form of Alzheimer's disease.

For this reason, I know little about my real father. You ask how I know this. Well, believe me, the information was not provided by anyone in the family. Flesh and blood did not reveal it to me, rather it was given to me by the Holy Ghost, yes that's right, it came from God himself. It happened during an Easter weekend while Mom and I prepared Easter dinner. From out of nowhere, the question came into my head. Ask your mother if your father is your real father? The thought was compelling and quite real to me. I simply asked her, Mom, is Daddy my real father? The answer was short and to the point. "Of course, he is."

I simply returned to what I was doing without questioning any further. However, about two hours later, she came to me and asked why I had asked the question. I told her that I didn't really know why. That's when the truth came out. She began to tell me the story of how I came to be, that the father who raised me as his own was not my real father. She told me everything and expressed great remorse. She said that she thought I would hate her. Quite to the contrary, I did not have any of those emotions. I just felt a form of relief.

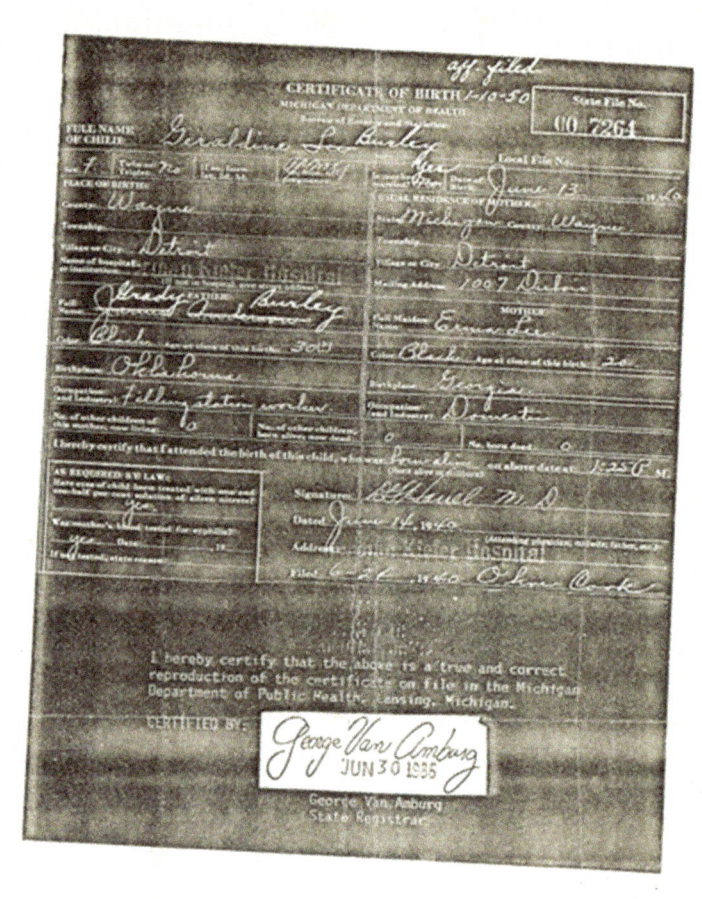

Please Note: I cannot find the original with the raised seal.

Certificate of Birth – Geraldine L. Burley - 1940

Chapter 8 – End the Beginning

Mom decided to plan a meeting through friends who knew of my biological father's whereabouts. To make a long story short, I met him only that one time. It was decided that because of his "lifestyle," as a gambler, he preferred that I not become a part of his life. I agreed to something that I later regretted. I have wondered about him for the rest of my life. As stated earlier, anything Mom may have known went with Alzheimer's disease.

I have come to realize that, by the mercy and grace of God, and the love of Christ, our lives were ordained by God from the foundation of the world for purpose. Although we may be in iniquity, our earthen vessels are formed through woundedness and challenges.

Against all odds, the forces of shame, disparity, depravity, and negativity we are God's beloved children. The character within us is miraculously strengthened and becomes disclaimers of pride and shame brought about through illegitimacy and ignorance. Though our purpose may be delayed, it will not be denied.

I surmise that families often feel their brokenness is unacceptable at church. Pain and a sense of failure are often well hidden by the deceptive fronts we maintain. It is crucial then for churches to communicate that there is no such thing as a "perfect Christian" no more than there is such a thing as a "perfect life." Because Christian families are simply families made up of individual Christians, what applies to one applies to the whole. I like this part – the good news – that *"while we still were sinners Christ died for us"* (Rom. 5:8).

Listen with me and you'll hear the precious sounds of our refusal to be hopeless, having an immovable and unshakable belief system rooted and grounded by faith. We find that the nature of brokenness is unacceptable.

Tabernacle Missionary Baptist Church – Detroit, MI

It bears repeating. Pain and a sense of failure are often hidden in the deceptive fronts that we maintain. All of us are earthen vessels. We are cracked, chipped, and sometimes quite broken. Therefore, I have come to realize that we are a people in denial who must recognize and acknowledge our shortcomings. Not only acknowledge but seek to rectify them through a sincere desire to break the bondage of denial.

Christian families, like the individual Christians of which they are comprised, are "simultaneously sinners and justified" (to use Luther's signature phrase). This means that they too have a high calling to pursue.

The world's wealth, power, prestige, and physical beauty are very seductive but ultimately illusory. They have no power to fulfill our deepest needs and great power to damage us not only spiritually, but emotionally and even physically. We now recognize that we are often operating as codependent, unconsciously reinforcing destructive behavior so that relationships become unhealthy. We need the church to proclaim and embody God's healing grace for the wounded inevitably inflicted by our compulsive attachment to worldly values.

It's difficult to avoid being touched in some way by the various components mentioned without becoming personally affected. Upon examination, you might find yourself being shaken to the core of reality.

Tabernacle Missionary Baptist Church – Detroit, MI

We are vehicles of grace to one another and although there is imperfection in us, God has graciously made us in "His Image." So even if you are weakened by death, divorce, physical disability, emotional problems, or economic hardship, you are still a living cell in the body of Christ. You have a mission to fulfill predestined by your anointed gifting. As I reflect on the whole point of this story, you will recall there was an element of REJECTION woven throughout.

SECTION THREE

BEYOND THE BLUE ROOM

Chapter 9 – Love at First Sight?

After falling and having to get back up, I realized that it was time for me to get serious about where my life was going. According to tradition, I was going to be married, so I visited the "old school theology," my next option.

Little did I know that my parents were intervening by getting me invited to a going away party at the home of one of their friends. Their nephew who had joined the army was commissioned to report for duty. In their mind, me going to this party seemed to be the perfect solution to the problem of meeting my husband. However, this idea took a turn. I didn't want to go to the party, but Mom and Dad insisted. I was dropped off and left to fend for myself.

When I arrived, I entered the house by going down the stairs that led to the basement where the party was being held. Upon arrival my eyes fell upon a good-looking young man from across the room that I had never met. It was love at first sight. I thought he was handsome and that I had died and gone to heaven. I just knew that he was to become my husband. I spoke it into existence, that he was to be my husband. Be careful what you ask for.

We became close almost immediately. Even though, I found out that he was there at the party with one of his many girlfriends, who "if looks could kill" they would have. This turned out to be another type of set up.

After a short period of time, I was asked to go on a date by this young man. This time we attended the wedding of his very best friend.

How romantic was that? That was when the generational curse reared its ugly head again. I did not recognize the red flags going up. Entrapment entered in for the kill.

We went to the wedding, and I had convinced myself that this was God ordained. Afterwards we began to see each other on a regular basis. I was so naive that I had no idea that my sweetheart was double dipping as well as tipping around. I was oblivious. I thought God had sent me the man of my dreams. But God works in mysterious ways, HIS wonders to perform.

Still young and uninformed, one day my boyfriend came to visit with sex on his mind. Again, having been sheltered and taught nothing but, keep your panties up and your skirt down, I was clueless as to what that really meant. So, when he approached me at home while my parents were away, I succumbed to the flesh. (*And when the woman saw that it was pleasant to the eyes, and a tree to be desired to make one wise, she took of the fruit thereof, and did eat, and gave also unto her husband with her, and he did eat. Genesis 3:6*) Indiscretion had entered in! The cover had come off.

Mr. & Mrs. John B. Callahan, Jr. - 1959

61

When I realized I was pregnant soon after, it wasn't a problem. We had discussed marriage, and I was already convinced that we were going to get married. Sounds familiar, end of story. According to me, it was already etched in stone. How blind can one be? *I once was lost, but now I'm found.* The pattern was beginning to form all over again. Grow up, go to school, get married, and live happily ever after. But God! *You meant evil against me; God meant it for good! (Genesis 50:20, NKJV). Be not overcome of evil. But overcome evil with good. (Romans 12:21 KJV)*

Wedding Party – Mr. & Mrs. John Callahan Sr, Reginald Callahan, Geraldine & John Callahan, Gloria McKenny, Mr. & Mrs. Grady B. Burley

After the secret was out, I dropped out of college to get married. We had a beautiful wedding at my parents' home, and a wonderful reception followed. The wakeup call came on the very night of the so-called honeymoon. When we finally found our way to our apartment, my husband was so drunk that he passed out on the sofa. I was waiting for him to come into the room and find me there, clothed in my beautiful lingerie. It did not happen. He was out cold. I slept alone in my bed on my wedding night. You would have thought that he would apologize, but instead this behavior continued during the weeks to come. He began staying out night after night with the boys getting drunk, even though the wedding celebration was over. This behavior overrode all the rituals that had been performed. It was a lie and a farce!

Chapter 10 – My Three Girls

Marriage has its share of ups and downs. It was a rocky road we traveled for 15 years ending in divorce. I'm most thankful for my three girls and extended family including in-laws. Mom, Dad, Aunts, Uncles and Cousins contributed to the village raising our children in the love of Jesus Christ. My girls received the solid foundation of love, joy, and peace because of the tribe of family. Days, weekends, and summer vacations were spent among the tribe. Cousins grew up more like siblings. There was a consistency in discipline among them all.

Amid marital trauma, I never worried about my girls. They were sheltered from all conflict because what happened behind closed didn't come to the light for many years. Closed door secrets remained just that. My three girls were cherished by all and treated like little princesses. They were not exposed to the struggles I endured.

Me and my three girls – Geraldine B. Callahan, Tjuana, Katrina & Yvette

In our home, the education of the children was a top priority. We were a two-parent working family. Structure and discipline were twin pillars. The home was well kept. Everyone had a part to play. Chores

Katrina, Yvette & Tjuana

were to be completed daily. Homework was not overlooked. We taught our girls good etiquette, high morals, and responsibility. We settled in a working-class neighborhood. The girls were able to build good relationships with other children there. It was a thriving family-oriented community.

The weekdays were scheduled structure. Weekends were wild recreation. But the tribe provided our girls with structured leisurely recreation. They were welcomed with open arms and full plates at several homes. Joyfully they bounced from Grandma to Uncle to Aunt to Grandma on any given weekend. Mom took them to church every week. Sunday dinner was a

Tjuana, Katrina & Yvette

family tradition at Mother-in-law's house.

Marriage was the standard in this tribe. The example of a stable marriage was exhibited by both of our parents. Always available through good and bad times, they were the strong backbone in our lives.

Holidays, birthdays, and special events were doubled as celebrations migrated from one grandparent's house to the other. Each

Me, Mom and my three girls – Geraldine B. Callahan, Erma L. Burley, Tjuana, Yvette & Katrina

celebration was uniquely grand.

We lived a prosperous life. The men of the family including Dad and Mom's brothers came together to build four vacation homes on one dirt road. They were constructed in a prominent resort area – Idlewild, Michigan. Every summer, all four houses were filled as we converged on the property for one or two weeks.

It was a time of fun, games, fishing, cooking, laughing and family games. Canasta was the game of choice. Until the wee hours of the morning, we were slamming cards on the table, talking loudly, and eating fish. There we were in the middle of the woods. No clocks to punch, no neighbors to disturb, we could be as loud as wanted. It was a great release. There were no phones to answer, no structure and no schedule. Just good, clean ole fashioned fun to be had by all. The girls were right there with their cousins. Running up and down the dirt roads by day. Playing their own games in their rooms by night. What a time! What a time! What – a – time.

Materially, we lacked for nothing. But mentally and spiritually I lacked peace of mind. Behind closed doors were the secrets that plagued my thoughts. After a while, they began to seep through the walls outside the room. I could no longer contain them. I had to escape. One fateful night, I packed my three girls into the car and went home to Mom and Dad. It had been 10 years too long when I decided to separate from my husband. The double life was just too much.

In the weekends of joy and laughter for our girls was turmoil and chaos in our marriage. My husband abandoned family life most weekends until Sunday dinner at his mom's house. I caroused with him till I could no longer enjoy for myself the wild parties, drinking and drug abuse. I became the butt of sneers and jokes. Losing my self-esteem, I no longer relished the company of my tall, dark, and handsome. I was intimidated and downright afraid because of our backroom lifestyle. I stopped participating in the weekend revels. But the revelry came home with him behind the closed doors of our room. The walls were closing in on me. With the desire to live for my three girls, I planned the way of escape and never returned.

Chapter 11 – The Great Escape

On that fateful night, I left with my girls across town with Mom and Dad. Moving back to the blue room was only a temporary fix. It was a safe haven. Here is where I could gather my thoughts about what's next. This was definitely not the final destination. Emotionally, I was still close enough to feel the effects of the collapsing walls. The mental stress was still overwhelming. Recuperation and recovery were needed to develop the strategy for the next chapter of life. The great escape would be executed in stages. I wanted to be far, far away.

Two-family flat in Detroit

Moving was an act of faith. Going back to my husband was not an option. We needed a place to live. By the grace and mercy of God, those doors opened in a two-family flat only a few blocks away from Mom. We occupied the flat upstairs. My girls transferred to schools in this area. There were adjustments to make. To our advantage, we were still in the immediate area of family. The support provided by extended family was vital in this transition. We settled there for a while.

This stage was a time to discover my identity and release the past of who I was if that makes any sense. Better stated, "Who am I now and where do I go from here?" Choosing to separate, I became a single parent without the support of my husband. This was a challenge for my girls and me. But we were in this together. Their foundation of home discipline was the base to build upon. They understood their responsibilities at school and at home. They looked out for each other. Grands, aunts, and uncles looked out for us all.

I was already working. Financially, I needed to build from this one income. God provided financial stability through employment. I needed to establish a budget, live within my means, and begin saving. There were sacrifices to be made. It was all worth it for my three girls. It would take patience, discipline, and a strategic plan to move on to the next stage. I consulted with friends and family members near and far.

Our tenure there was about a year. Then a vision took root in my mind talking to an aunt in Atlanta who encouraged me to move there. "Come to Atlanta," she said. She assured me that she would give us a place to get started. As a child, I spent many summers in Georgia. There are supportive aunts and cousins in Atlanta. We won't be totally alone, but we will be far, far away. This would be the great escape. Even though the destination was secure in my mind, an abrupt move was not wise. Now came the time of release. This meant a total break from Detroit to move to Atlanta.

I released possessions by selling or giving things I could not or would not take to Atlanta. Over time, our property was reduced to clothes, bedding, and small household items. Heart-to-heart talks with closest family and friends were the initial release of deep personal relationships. I would no longer be down the street and around the corner. We were leaving the close-knit support circle for another circle. Atlanta is more than 700 miles away. We would be releasing the northern lifestyle for the South. I was moving my girls from everything they knew and held dear, believing that in the long run our lives would be better.

With the help of cousins and friends, I placed applications for employment in Atlanta. My resume was marketable with Clerical, Secretarial and Administrative expertise. My skills were impressive, and my career was established. I was a valuable asset in any office. My work ethics had already been proven. Before long, airline tickets were purchased for in person interviews. Finally, the job was secured. It was time to move.

All our possessions were packed into a U-Haul trailer. The trailer was attached to the bumper of our small Mercury Cougar. Early the next morning, we quickly got into the car and left. The day of departure was full of adrenaline. The girls had not been informed about the plan. They had no idea where we were going before the sudden awakening. Somehow, my husband got wind of it. He appeared angry, and emotional with intimidating threats. But I would not be deterred. I drove away with my girls heading toward I-75 to Atlanta.

It was a long, complicated ride with mishaps along the way. It was not without the support of an uncle who came as driver and protector. With every mile, we were leaving the past behind; leaving Detroit behind; leaving our family behind. It seemed like forever. Praise God for leading and providing all the way!

We had crossed well into Ohio when the trailer detached from the car taking the bumper with it. Thank the Lord, there were no cars in its path! The trailer stopped hitting a tree on the side of the highway. I was relieved and disturbed at the same time. Relieved because the trailer seemed to be intact. Disturbed because all our stuff was there attached to a tree instead of the car.

We were stuck on the side of the highway in need of reinforcements. There was no phone or phone booth nearby. Through the trees, there was a building in walking distance. I was able to call home. Two more uncles came flying down the highway to our rescue.

After a hotel stay, obtaining a new bumper, a proper trailer hitch and getting the needed repair we were able to forge ahead. But that would not take place without examining the content of the trailer. The weight must be evenly distributed for smooth transportation. The calvary returned to Detroit. We continued safely on to Atlanta.

Because of careful preparation, an apartment was ready for us. The job awaited me there. The great escape was fulfilled; we were here to stay. Ironically, I moved to Georgia where this story begins, the home of Mom and Dad.

My three girls & me – Yvette, Tjuana, Katrina & Geraldine B. Callahan

The escape was final mentally, physically, and emotionally. I had no fear of collapsing walls, intimidating threats, and the emotional roller coasters of my past. My feet were squarely planted in Atlanta. With freedom in sight, there were new adventures to explore. I knew we would be alright.

Chapter 12 – Destiny Meets Purpose

I left Mom, Dad, and in-laws in Detroit. Yet, they were only a phone call away. I was a single parent all the way. There was an extended family in Atlanta who was the catalyst to my success. I Thank God for them all. For me, it was a clean break; a sever. With great satisfaction, I can say this is where I flourished.

Within just a few months, God provided a house through a homeowner's assistance program for single parents. When we move in faith, God does miraculous things. We were blessed with a stable home well beyond their high school years. This was culture shock for all of us. Streets and neighborhoods are different. The school system was a definite adjustment for the girls. There was no integration in Detroit schools. We discovered that the school system was behind in Atlanta. They made the necessary adjustments to matriculate through school academically and socially stable.

The girls spent entire summers in Detroit throughout their high school years. They were able to reunite with their dad, beloved grandparents, aunts, uncles, and cousins. It was a blessing to them and to me as well. I didn't have to be concerned about my girls all day while I was working. Every year in June, each had their own suitcase in which they packed all their clothes. We put them on a Delta flight back home. They returned to Atlanta at the end of August just in time for the next school year. Freedom, freedom, OH FREEDOM!

The launching pad of my career in Atlanta was a Data Entry Clerk at a major railroad company. From there, the door opened wide at a local recreation center in the position of secretary. My work ethics were superb. I was always looking for a better opportunity. That prospect revealed itself in the mayor's office. A paradigm shift took place. God promoted me from a small recreation center to city hall working with the movers and the shakers of Atlanta. From secretary to administrative assistant to executive assistant, I worked under four dynamic mayoral administrations in my career. These iconic mayors were Mayors Sam Massel, Maynard Jackson, Andrew Young, and Bill Campbell. Soaring with the eagles, God entrusted me with a very influential role.

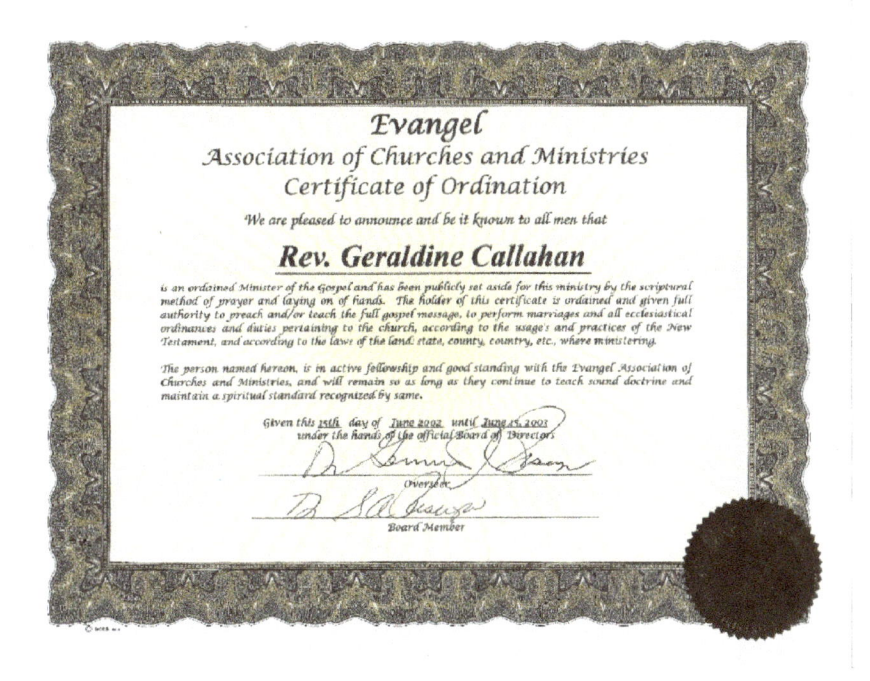

If that wasn't high enough, God would take me even higher. Hearing the call of Jesus Christ, I said Yes Lord! The journey began in a local Bible institute in the church where I attended. Women in ministry were not popular nor widely accepted. Yet when I sought God for what He wanted me to do I heard, "Preach the Gospel." I was shocked. I hadn't even considered this. Of all the gifts and talents, preaching wasn't in my vocabulary. By faith, I boldly moved forward. If God be for me, who can be against me. Ministry begins at home. Within a few years, it became necessary for me to retire from the city to take care of Mom and Dad in Detroit. Mom was diagnosed with Alzheimer's disease. Dad could no longer care for her on his own. This was a major transition. I cared for them the next 8 years till first Mom and then Dad transitioned from this life to be with the Lord.

Mom & Dad – Erma L. Burley & Grady B. Buley

God shifted my scope and perspective completely. He promoted me from City Hall to His Holy Empire, the Kingdom of God. This was my training ground. It was not easy watching the decline of Mom. Enduring attacks of the enemy day and night was excruciating. This was spiritual warfare. What a mighty God we serve!

I returned to membership in the church of my youth this time to serve, to teach and to minister to like-minded singles. I served on the ministerial staff of dozens under the leadership of a mighty warrior, Dr. Frederick G. Sampson. I learned to depend on the guidance of the

Holy Spirit. The seminary education continued in Detroit where God blessed me with Master of Divinity at the age of 62. He gets all the praise, honor, and glory!

Graduation Picture – Destiny Christian University - 2006

Even though I left my girls in Atlanta, I gained so many more sons and daughters in the family of God. My passion was Singles Ministry. The approach was to be satisfied in Jesus as a single person. This was not a dating program in the church. Teaching the word of God was the main objective. God poured so much into me as a single woman and a single parent. To whom much is given, much is required. The God of all comfort blessed me. That anointing is for others. Blessed to be a blessing, I had so much to offer in Jesus.

Rev. Geraldine B. Callahan preaching at Tabernacle -2001

    1 Corinthians 7:32 -35 encourages the unmarried to have an undivided devotion to the Lord. Paul also admonishes that those who are married have a divided interest in how to please their spouse. Teaching was focused on being single, whole at one with Christ. Being single is not a deficit. Our relationship with Christ makes us complete. This firm confirmation leads to healthy godly relationships in every other area of life. Faith, prayer, repentance, salvation, and the grace of God is the foundation on which we stand.

Fondest memories reside in mission trips to the Bahamas Islands. A team of ministers were sent from the church every summer. Four years, I was privileged to join the team. What joy, what contentment, what excitement we experienced. I was primed with low expectations to preach on the island because a female preacher was definitely taboo. Serving the children on the small remote islands was a source of pride. They were so precious. Teaching about the love of Jesus brought so much joy. I was humbled and honored to do just that. Coming back to the main island, attending worship services there was moving, and spirit filled. The celebratory parades were grand. I knew we had become one with this move, when we were invited to march in their parade. We marched glowing in the Spirit, holding our banners, grinning from ear to ear. The pinnacle of praise came when, despite tradition of men, I was asked to preach. Hallelujah! Glory to God! Praise Him!

Rev. Geraldine B. Callahan

The training ground was watered with tears of joy, pain, and anguish. In her final years, caring for Mom was increasingly demanding. Dad and I were no longer able to provide what she needed at home. The decision was made to place her in a nursing home. It broke my heart. Visiting her every day brought me only a small consolation. Her final day came much sooner than I expected. But then I could never really be prepared to see her go. I questioned the decision made to place her in the nursing home. My only comfort was, "God knows best. He never makes a mistake."

Now, it was me and Dad. I cared for him for two more years. He was in pretty good health until a mass developed on his jar. At his age, he decided not to have it removed. It was a slow progressive tumor that brought him to his dying day. He took me in as his own. He was truly a father to me. Truly I was blessed to have him as a father. After his death I closed the doors of this house for good and move back to Atlanta.

A sinner saved by grace, life has been filled with ups and downs. As with all humans, perfection is not obtained. I've come this far by faith leaning on the Lord. Trusting in His holy word. He hasn't failed me yet. Though I only met my biological father once, the gambling trait was in my blood. It plagued me for many years. Thank God for the blood of Jesus who delivered me. I haven't married again. Relationships have been good, great, disappointing, and even devastating. But God remained faithful in His commitment to loving me. I love Him, I love Him, yes, I do.

I'll make this the last chapter even though I could go on. Where destiny meets purpose, we sing our final song. God ordered my steps. I answered His call. Praise God! Hallelujah! Thank God for saving me.

Mom, Dad & Me – Erma. Grady & Geraldine

CITY OF ATLANTA

MAYNARD JACKSON
MAYOR

30 July 1990

Ms. Gerrie Callahan
Office of the Mayor
55 Trinity Avenue, S.W., Suite 2400
Atlanta, Georgia 30335

Dear Gerrie:

Many thanks for your contribution in participating on the Planning Committee for the Nelson Mandela Freedom Fund Tour.

Your efforts were truly valuable to the success of Atlanta's tribute to Deputy President and Mrs. Mandela and the African National Congress delegation -- a day which forever will be remembered for its historical significance to Atlanta in the struggle for human rights and for the symbolic unification in the struggle to end Apartheid in South Africa.

Best wishes and sincere thanks. You served your city well.

Yours for Atlanta,

Maynard Jackson

MHJ/vbj

Letter of Thanks from Mayor Maynard Jackson - 1990

Geraldine B. Callahan

Geraldine B. Callahan

CITY OF ATLANTA
55 TRINITY AVENUE, S.W.
ATLANTA, GEORGIA 30335-0300
(404) 330-6100

BILL CAMPBELL
MAYOR

August 7, 1996

Geraldine Callahan
Housing & Community Development

Dear Geraldine:

Congratulations on a job well done as host of the 1996 Centennial Olympic Games! Our City looks great and we have responded extremely well to the needs of both citizens and visitors.

I know that to accomplish this high level of service, you worked extremely hard and sacrificed a great deal. For that reason, I want to express how proud I am of you and to offer sincere thanks for what you and your co-workers have done.

The demands of the Games gave us the opportunity to learn some lessons about the value of advance planning, a focus on customer service, team work, and valuing our employees. Our challenge is to maintain the high levels of service delivery, team work, civic pride and enthusiasm we have displayed during the Olympic Games.

Because of employees such as you, our streets and parks were kept clean, our Water Department met our expectations and as promised, our service delivery to our non-Olympic neighborhoods was not diminished. Hartsfield International Airport effectively handled the increased passenger flow and the emergency services, and public safety personnel responded magnificently even in the face of tragedy.

A special thanks goes to the employees who came forward to help in areas outside of their traditional work arena such as responding to citizens requests in the Mayor's 24-hour Operations Center or working as Special Enforcement Officers to enforce vending laws.

Again thank you for the phenomenal work you've performed. The citizens of Atlanta and I appreciate what you have accomplished.

Sincerely,

Bill Campbell

Letter of Thanks from Mayor Bill Campbell - 1996

My three girls – Yvette Stanley, Katrina Peek, & Tjuana Callahan - 2018

Geraldine B. Callahan - 2018

Geraldine B. Callahan with John B. Callahan - 2019

My three girls – Tjuana Callahan, Katrina Peek & Yvette Stanley - 2022

About the Authors

<u>Reverend Geraldine Callahan</u>

A hardworking independent woman who endured the struggles of humanity in this world amidst various trials.
A bold woman willing to relocate from Detroit to Atlanta with her three school age daughters in the '70s.
A mover and a shaker whose administrative skills made a difference and promoted her to City Hall.
A team player in the Atlanta Mayor's Office from 1974 – 1996.
A pacesetter and trend setter, prepared by God and anointed to preach the gospel.
A dedicated teacher, preacher, evangelist, missionary, pastor, and apostle of Jesus Christ.
A disciple of Jesus Christ who studied to show herself approved.
A warrior who fought the good fight of faith.
A trailblazer who forged a path for women aspiring to preach in the pulpit with the same respect as men.
A woman of excellence inspiring other servants.
An author and orator, confident and bold mouthpiece for the Lord.

<u>Tjuana Ladawn Callahan</u>

A retired State of Georgia employee who served 1979 - 2013 in the field of accounting.
A mother of three who dedicates her life to family.
A disciple of Jesus Christ.
A member of New Morning Light Baptist Church 1993 to date.
A writer of poetry, short stories, prayers, songs, plays and essays.
A woman who uses the gift of prophesy in inspirational spoken word expression.
A Bible teacher for children 1993 – 2010 and adults to date.
A 12-Step support group leader 2011 – 2023.

Other books by the Authors:

Write the Vision – Author: Gerrie Callahan

The Seedline: Old Testament Survey – Author: Dr. Grant R. Carter with Dr. Geraldine Callahan as Editor, Publisher, and Cover Design

Remembering "Doc" – Author: Dr. Geraldine Callahan

Ain't God Good! – Author: Tjuana Ladawn Callahan

Moving Out of Dream Castles, Where Dreams Become Reality – Author: Tjuana Ladawn Callahan-Stewart

The Love Life of Fear and Paranoia – Author: Tjuana Ladawn Callahan

Inkwells: Dips and Drips of Life's Wisdom – Author: Sage Elders – A Compilation of Dr. Geraldine Callahan, Tjuana Ladawn Callahan, Carol D. Dye, Ruby Finney, Patricia Ann Callahan Morris, Annette Tooks, Denise Vicks, and Donna J. Ware

Inkwell: Dips and Drips of Life's Journeys – Author: Sage Elders – A Compilation of Dr. Geraldine Callahan, Tjuana Ladawn Callahan, Lillian S. Collins, Carol D. Dye, Ruby Finney, Trudie V. Lee, Patricia Ann Callahan Morris, Annette Tooks, Denise Vicks, and Donna J. Ware

Picture References

Introduction

The Blue Room – Geraldine's room

The Blue Room – Geraldine's room

Chapter 1

Grandpa, Grandma, Uncle & Mom – Mitchell L. Lee, Sr, Pearl Bell Easton Lee, James Lee & Erma Lee

Grandpa & Grandma - Mitchell L. Lee, Sr & Pearl Bell Easton Lee

Children at the home house in Eatonton, GA

Family History written by Patience Ordell Lee Singleton – 1986

Chapter 2

Home House in Eatonton, GA

Mom – Erma Lee

Mom – Erma Lee

Chapter 3

Mitchell Lee Jr.

James Lee, Mitchell Lee & friend

Chapter 4

Mom & Dad – Erma L. Burley & Grady B. Burley

Geraldine Lee Burley

Chapter 5

Family Picture – Me, Mom, Uncles & Cousins - 1958

Our Home in Detroit, MI

Warranty Deed – Our home in Detroit, MI - 1950

Chapter 6

Geraldine L. Burley

Gloria McKenney & Geraldine L. Burley

Ladies' Club – Friends with Geraldine L. Burley

Singing Group – Joe Stubbs & The Falcons - 1958

Geraldine L. Burley

Recording Agreement – Kudo Recording Associates 1958

Chapter 7

Certificate of Birth – Geraldine L. Burley - 1940

Chapter 8

Our Church in Detroit – Tabernacle Missionary Baptist Church

Our Church in Detroit – Tabernacle Missionary Baptist Church

Chapter 9

Wedding – Mr. & Mrs. John B. Callahan, Jr. - 1959

Wedding Party – John B. Callahan Sr, Vivian Callahan, Reginald Callahan, Geraldine & John Callahan, Gloria McKenny, Grady B. Burley & Erma L. Burley

Chapter 10

Me and my three girls – Geraldine B. Callahan, Tjuana, Katrina & Yvette

Katrina, Yvette & Tjuana

Tjuana, Yvette & Katrina

Me, Mom and my three girls – Geraldine B. Callahan, Erma L. Burley, Tjuana, Yvette & Katrina

Chapter 11

Two-family flat in Detroit

My three girl & me –Yvette, Tjuana, Katrina & Geraldine B. Callahan

Chapter 12

Mom & Dad – Erma L. Burley & Grady B. Burley

Certificate of Ordination – Rev. Geraldine B. Callahan – 2002

Graduation Picture – Destiny Christian University – 2006

Rev. Geraldine B. Callahan preaching at Tabernacle Missionary Baptist Church - 2001

Rev. Geraldine B. Callahan

Mom & Dad with Me – Erma L. Burley, Grady B. Burley & Geraldine B. Callahan

Me & Dad – Geraldine B. Callahan & Grady B. Burley

Letter of Thanks from Mayor Maynard Jackson - 1990

Geraldine B. Callahan

Geraldine B. Callahan

Letter of Thanks from Mayor Bill Campbell - 1996

My three girls – Yvette Stanley, Katrina Peek & Tjuana Callahan - 2018

Geraldine B. Callahan – 2018

Geraldine B. Callahan with John B. Callahan, Jr - 2019

My three girls – Tjuana Callahan, Katrina Peek & Yvette Stanley – 2022